Johnny Joey Jones
Blown Away Coloring Book
Copyright © 2017 Dabel Brothers Publishing
Copyright © 2017 Johnny Joey Jones

All rights reserved. Published by Dabel Brothers Publishing. No part of this book
maybe reproduced or transmitted in any form or by any means, electronic or mechanical,
including photocopying, recording, or by any information storage and retrieval system,
without written permission from the publisher.

For information address Dabel Brothers Publishing,
3330 Cobb Parkway, Ste #324-245, Acworth, GA 30101
www.dabelbrothers.com

Consulting editor: David Campiti
Book design by Les Dabel
Cover art by Michael Montenat & Manuel Preitano
Interior art by Glass House Graphics' Michael Montenat, Ricardo Jaime, Rod Rodollfo,
Mel Joy San Juan, & Manuel Preitano

ISBN: 978-0-9996163-0-7

Printed in the United States of America

Tips on how to color this Coloring Book:

Thank you for purchasing this Dabel Brothers Coloring Book.

It's one of many Coloring Books we currently have available from your favorite authors, book series, TV shows, movies, games, Musicians... the list goes on and will continue to grow as we add more amazing Coloring Books to our lineup.

If you enjoyed this Coloring Book please make sure to post your colored pages on our social media and leave us a review. We also encourage you to purchase a copy for your loved ones, as coloring is a great source of stress relief.

Make sure to visit our website DabelBrothers.com for news on upcoming titles and free goodies.

Yours Truly,

Dabel Brothers

1 Always test any markers before you start coloring, using the test page in the back of the book to see if the marker bleeds through or leaves a shadow.

2 If you are using a marker, paint or watercolor pencils. Slip a piece of paper behind the page your are coloring to protect the pages behind from bleed through issues.

3 Have LOTS of fun coloring and always remember, coloring is twice as fun when you are coloring with others. So make sure you have plenty of copies of this book for you and your loved ones :)

Hello!

My name is Johnny Joey Jones, but please call me Joey. Or Sgt Jones. Or JJ. Or Triple J! Thank you for taking a brief tour of my journey through the pages of this coloring book! I had the pleasure of serving you and all Americans as an EOD or Bomb Technician in the United States Marine Corps.

I left a small North Georgia town in 2005 and served in places like Afghanistan and Iraq until I finally retired in 2012. Like most service, mine came with a little bit of sacrifice; the loss of both legs in Afghanistan in 2010. Although I suffered a pretty severe injury, I can tell you, as a United States Marine... I had one bad day!

I hope coloring these scenes depicting my life as a Marine, my injury and recovery, as well as some amazing opportunities afterwards helps you see that everyone can endure adversity and find a fun, meaningful life!

Ooh-Rah!
Triple J

The "Buzzard, Bomb, and Pick" is one of the very few artistic designs used to identify a unit or job field in the United States Marine Corps. Unlike the Army, the Marine Corps doesn't wear any patches on the sleeves of its uniform and allows very few badges to be worn on combat utilities. This design is a friendly parody of the Eagle, Globe, and Anchor and represents the lonely and often under-supported duty of a bomb technician. This symbol has represented the most dangerous job in the United State Marine Corps since 1968.

Most EOD teams are made of 3 technicians. When we landed in Afghanistan in 2010, the IEDs were so prevalent and the roads were so restricting compared to Iraq, that we had to work in 2-man teams and had almost 4 times as many EOD techs per battalion of Infantry Marines. For a 2 week period in June, I worked with Team "Road House".

"Dude, when I first got here I couldn't wait to work my next IED. Now, looking at the calendar, I just hope I don't have to work too many more and get home in one piece."

—Sgt Mesa (far left)

We were transported from base-to-base by helicopter. The CH-53 or "Sea Stallion" is the workhorse of the Marine Corps. The back of the aircraft is always left open with a Marine sitting behind a .50 caliber machine gun.

"Don't worry about all that oil leaking on your gear. If these things aint leak'n, something's broke!"

—Anonymous Marine, (*door gunner*)

We always try to disarm or render safe IEDs using tools like robots from a safe distance. However, the terrain and lack of infrastructure in Helmand, Afghanistan meant we usually were doing it by hand. The worst-case scenario became common practice in the summer of 2010.

"Don't go looking to be a hero. A lot of guys count IEDs and think that means something. In this place, if you've worked one IED, you're as much an EOD tech as the guy who had to do 100. Just be smart and go home alive."

—GySgt Floyd Holley, (*KIA AFG 2010*)

After a long 2-day operation with a few casualty evacuations, getting ambushed multiple times, and getting lucky a few times as well, we were able to take a rest as we regrouped our platoon of Marines and exited the village we'd fought through to rescue Marines.

"Some people spend an entire lifetime wondering if they made a difference in the world. But, the Marines don't have that problem."

—President Ronald Reagan

On August 6th 2010 in the Garmsir district of the Helmand Province of Afghanistan in a small village called "Safar Bazaar," my luck ran out. I stepped on and was blown up by an IED.

"The first words Jones said were' Sorry I screwed up, Sir.' I couldn't understand why he was sorry. He'd just lost his legs. I saw him years later, smiling with his family. Then I finally got it, no apology required."

—Terry McCarthy CBS News, (*Embed reporter*)

MEANING OF THE EXPLOSIVE ORDNANCE DISPOSAL BADGE

THE WREATH is symbolic of the achievements and laurels gained by minimizing accident potentials through the ingenuity and devotion to duty of its members. It is in memory of the EOD personnel who have given their lives while performing EOD duties.

THE BOMB was copied from the design of the World War II Bomb Disposal Badge. The bomb represents the historic and major objective of the EOD attack, the unexploded bomb. The 3 fins represent the major areas of nuclear, conventional, and chemical/biological warfare.

THE LIGHTNING BOLTS symbolize the potential destructive power of the bomb and the courage and professionalism of EOD personnel in their endeavors to reduce hazards as well as to render explosive ordnance harmless.

THE SHIELD represents the EOD mission, which is to protect personnel and property in the immediate area from an inadvertent detonation of hazardous ordnance.

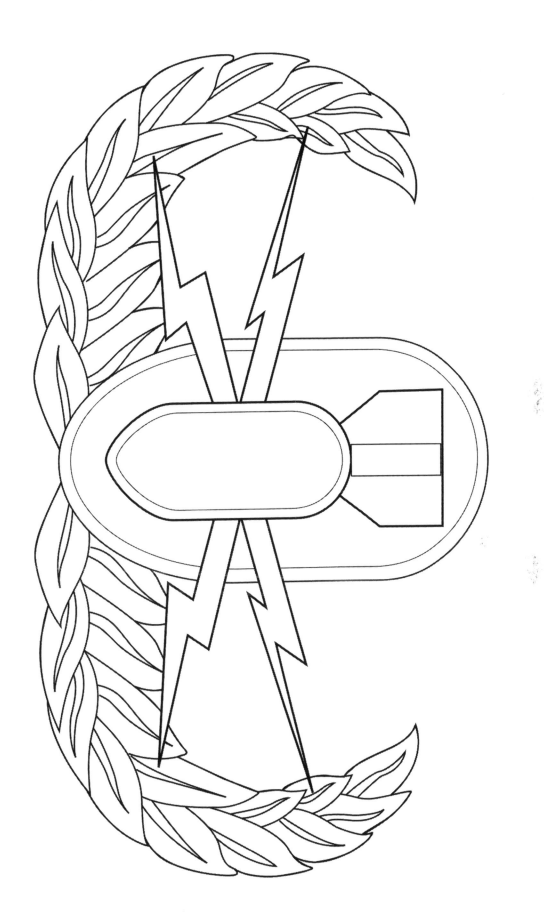

"THE LONG WALK"

The "Long Walk" is what we call the experience of walking down on your first bomb. Whether it's a conventional mortar hung in a launching tube, a grenade down-range that didn't explode, or an IED in Iraq or Afghanistan, in almost every situation that requires EOD support, a tech has to walk down and check it out or take an action. We always take that walk alone and the first time is always the most exciting and most stressful.

W hen I finally landed at Walter Reed Army Medical Center on August 10th 2010, I was one of only a handful of severely-wounded or amputated Marines in the now well-known 5th Floor Ward. By September, there were dozens and by October, more than 50. Dozens of them were EOD technicians I served with. 2010 and 2011 were the deadliest years of the War On Terror for the Marine Corps.

"You've been told that you're broken, that you're damaged goods, and should be labeled victims (PTSD) of two unjust and poorly executed wars. The truth, instead, is that we are the only folks with the skills, determination, and values to ensure American dominance in this chaotic world. There is also Post-Traumatic Growth. You come back from war stronger and more sure of who you are."

—General James Mattis, Secretary of Defense

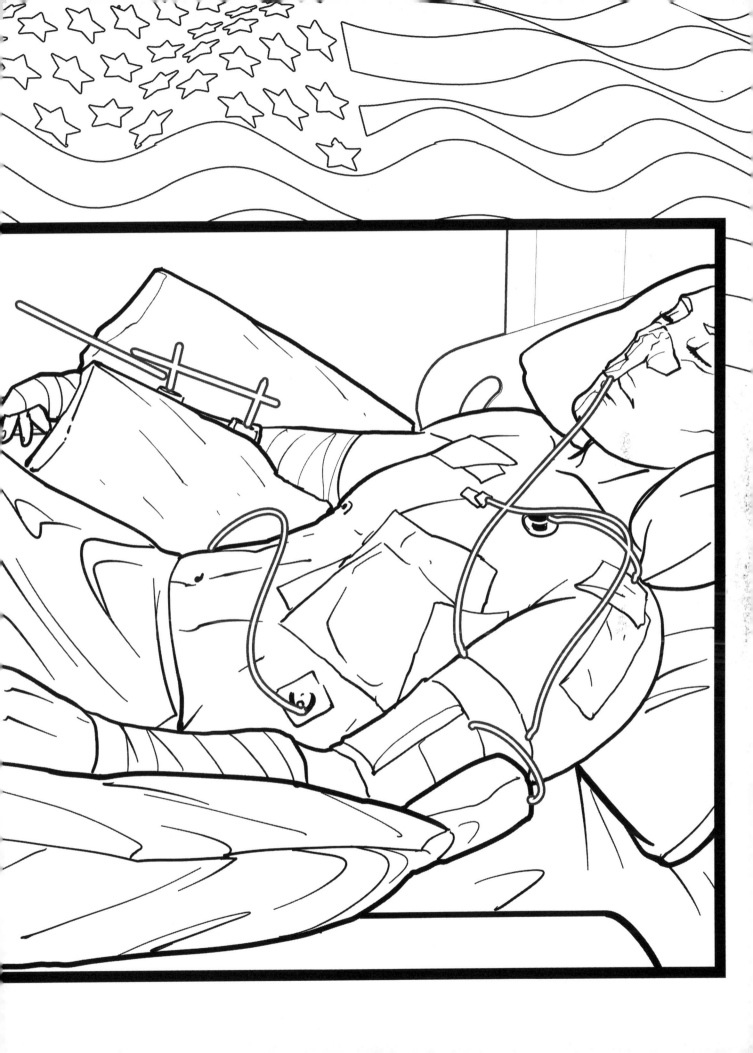

Some people will set a glass of water in front of you and tell you that perspective is looking at that glass and asking yourself if it is half empty or half full. I'm here to tell you that what matters, perspective, is looking at that glass and asking yourself if you are filling it up or pouring it out. It's not the situation you're given, but how you respond to it.

—Johnny Joey Jones

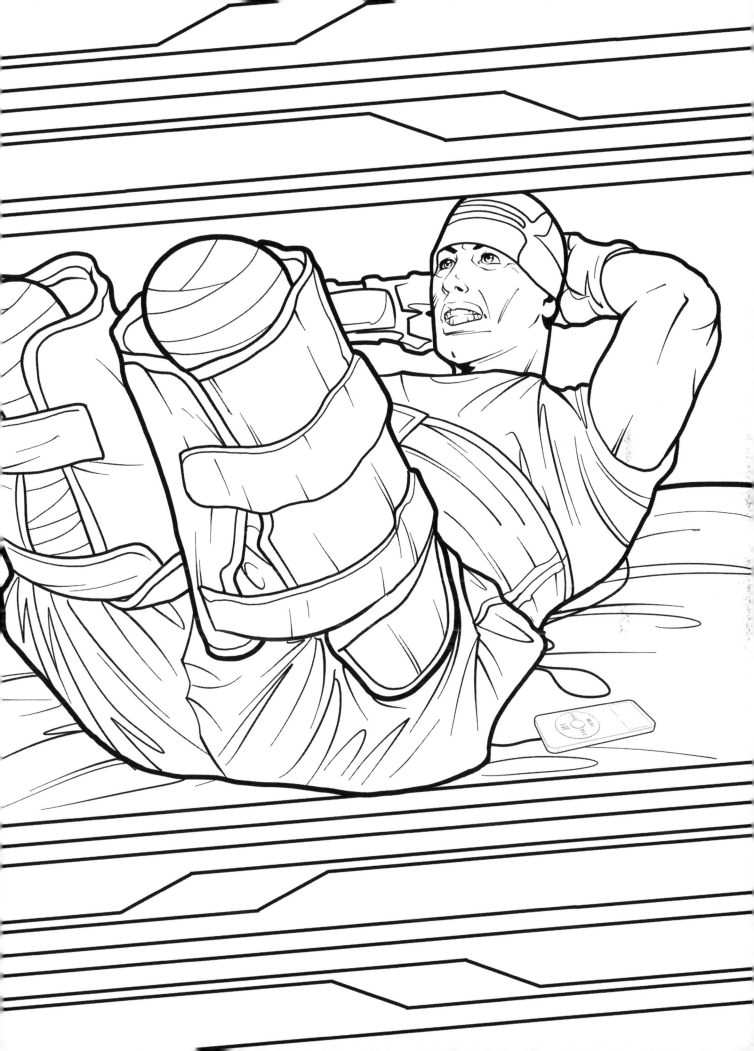

I used to visit the newly injured Marines and Sailors every Thursday evening after I began walking on prosthetic legs. It was important to me that they see what was next for them. Most of them were still healing and wouldn't be exposed to prosthetics for a few more weeks. I decided to bring the visual of a guy who'd been through what they were going through and was literally walking in their door. I'd tell them:

"It's not by choice that you lost your legs and it's not your choice to be in that bed or in that wheelchair, or one day on these legs, but what you do from that bed, wheelchair, or legs is 100% up to you. You can live a full life after this if you choose to. It's only up to you!"

—Johnny Joey Jones

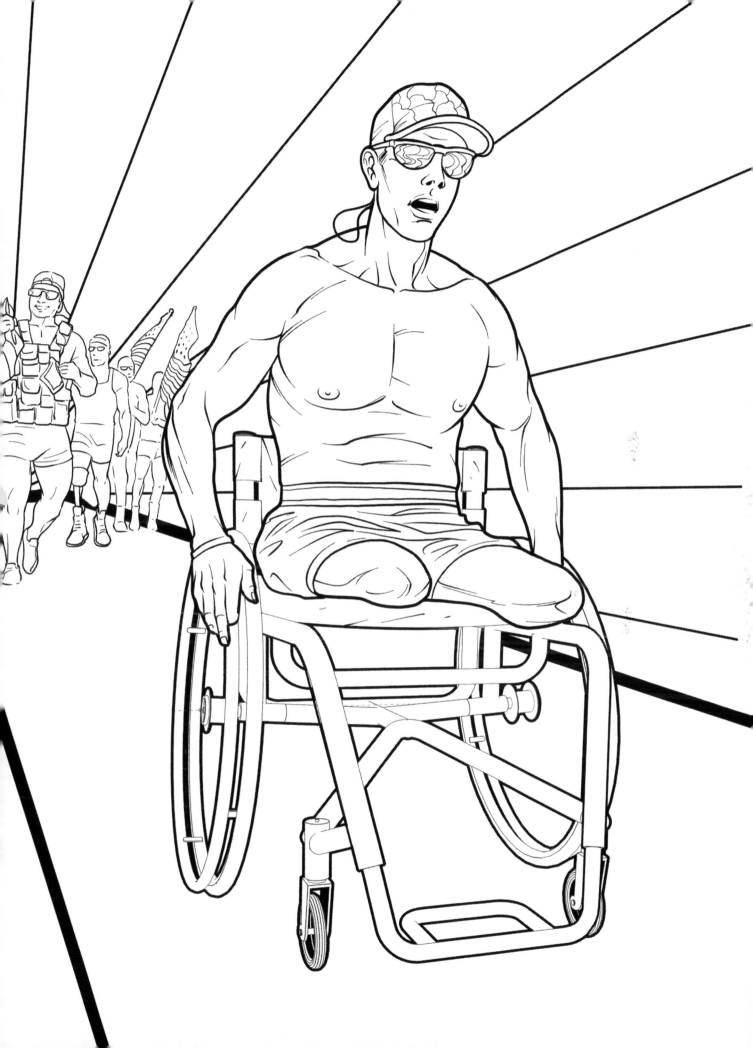

I was injured in August 2010. I began walking in February 2011 and going to school, volunteering, and working full-time in Congress in July 2011. Ten and a half months after getting blown away, I'd decided to not let a simple injury define or restrict who I was and what I was going to do with my life.

Much of the work I did while deployed was performed with the assistance of bomb-sniffing dogs. The true effect of these dogs when fully integrated into combat units is hard to describe. Yes, they are there to work, but they also serve a greater purpose – to remind us of the innocence we're fighting for while enduring the harshest throes of chaos. My dog Tucker, has been a tremendous blessing in my life.

In 2012 I was asked by then-Commandant of the Marine Corps, General James Amos, to speak on behalf of all combat wounded Marines as the Guest of Honor at the 2012 Marine Corps' Birthday Dinner in Washington D.C. This honor was one shared with past Members of Congress, Secretaries of Defense, and Medal of Honor recipients. Although one of the proudest moments in my life, I was there to speak for thousands of Marines who'd paid a great price. I had one message to deliver to the 3,500 distinguished Marines and public figures in attendance...

"As combat wounded Marines, remember this: WE are not limited, We are adaptive. WE are not victims, WE are survivors. And WE are not the resentment of this War on Terror, but the resilience of it!"

I met President George W. Bush in 2014. He was charismatic and fun. The first thing he asked me was "How's your head?" Meaning, "are you struggling with PTSD?" President Bush is of a similar notion that many of us share; Post-Traumatic Stress doesn't always have to be a disorder.

"Most of us imagine if the moment called for it that we would risk our lives to protect a spouse or a child. Those wearing the uniform assume that risk for the safety of strangers."

—President George W. Bush

Out of the night that covers me,
Black as the pit from pole to pole,
I thank whatever gods may be
For my unconquerable soul.

In the fell clutch of circumstance
I have not winced nor cried aloud.
Under the bludgeonings of chance
My head is bloody, but unbowed.

Beyond this place of wrath and tears
Looms but the Horror of the shade,
And yet the menace of the years
Finds, and shall find me, unafraid.

It matters not how strait the gate,
How charged with punishments the scroll,
I am the master of my fate:
I am the captain of my soul.

—William Ernest Henley

After my injury and recovery, I found purpose in helping my brothers and sisters-in-arms. Although many people focus on the loss of my legs, I would say I'm certainly more blessed now than I've ever been and the small sacrifices I've made have only made me a stronger and more dedicated patriot to the people I share this country with!

In 2012 I was invited to dine with President Obama, Vice President Biden, the Secretary of Defense, and 34 of the 36 Four-Star Generals serving in the U.S. armed forces at that time. Being the only Noncommissioned Officer at the Combatant Commanders dinner was an incredible honor. At one point President Obama asked me, "If you were back there in Afghanistan right now, what would you do differently?" Having never lost my ill-timed sense of humor, I replied, "I'd step left instead of right."

"So long as I'm Commander-in-Chief, we will sustain the strongest military the world has ever known. When you take off the uniform, we will serve you as well as you've served us because no one who fights for this country should have to fight for a job, or a roof over their head, or the care that they need when they come home."

—President Barack Obama

The disputed history and lore of challenge coins varies from Roman Legions to World War One American fighter pilots. Like many military traditions, the facts aren't as important as the meaning. Today, challenge coins in the military are often used by commanding officers and senior enlisted as a way of spontaneously recognizing rank and file who display good discipline and character. When a Marine, Soldier, Sailor, or Airman, receives a challenge coin, he or she carries that coin on them all the time. The "challenge" usually refers to the tradition of placing your coin on a bar when drinking with fellow service members. If the person you challenge can produce a higher ranking or rarer coin at that moment, then you owe them a beer. If not, they owe you one!

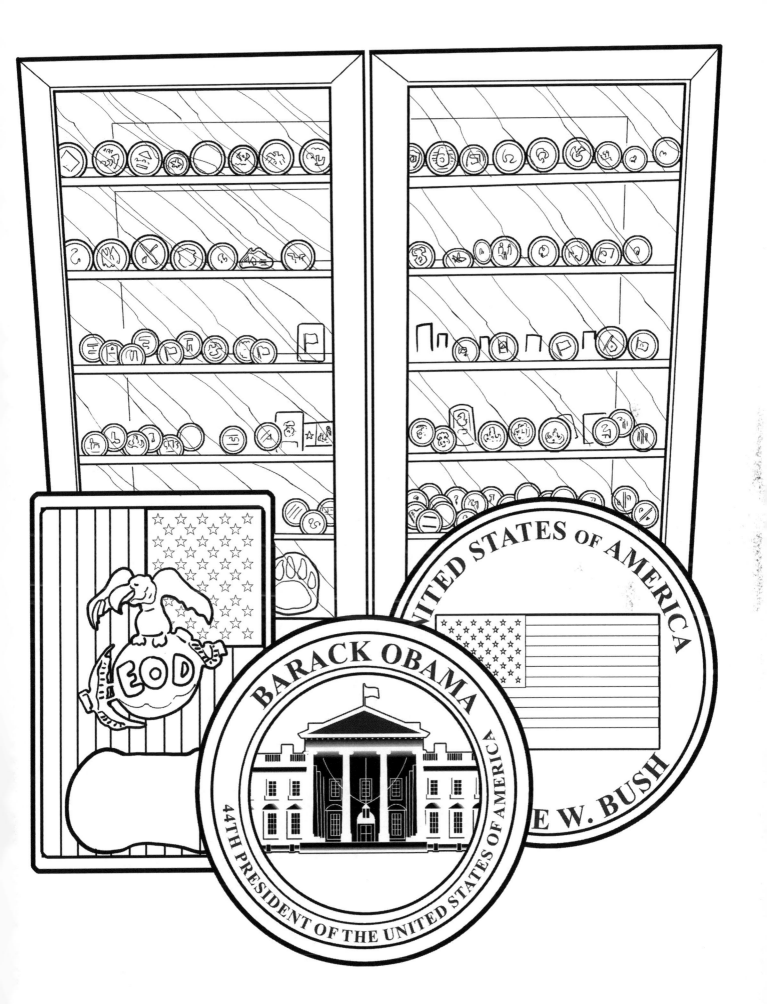

We often refer to WWII veterans as "America's Greatest Generation" seeing as how they saved the United States and its allies from the most formidable villain in our history only to come home and propel the American economy to the forefront of modern business. I'd say it's a pretty fitting moniker. I had the pleasure of meeting many WWII veterans at Arlington National Cemetery in 2014 while working in Washington D.C. as they visited their own memorial and fallen brothers on an Honor Flight.

"Uncommon valor was a common virtue."

—Admiral Chester Nimitz, in Iwo Jima, 1945

Since 2016, I have worked with one of the smartest, most talented, and patriotic groups of people I know, here at Camp Southern Ground. Zac Brown of Zac Brown Band is a dear friend and founder.

"Our Veterans that have given an incredible amount, who have given a lot of their lives and some of their soul for us... we have to help bring their mind and heart back home."

—Zac Brown, Camp Southern Ground

My Son was born just months before I left for Afghanistan. During my recovery, he was an incredible source of motivation to regain independence and happiness. I wrote this poem to show him how much of an inspiration he has been for me.

A Note to My Boy:

Let me tell you something son
about who your daddy is
so rough around the edges
oh, where to begin

Mistakes, he's made so many
but with you, he got it right
unplanned, unexpected maybe
but he'll often say, "that boy saved my life"

For so long, so reckless
you could say he lost his way
but when you're walking behind him
he knows he must walk straight

Some people would call him a hero
for doing what any man should
Son your daddy is no hero,
Just wants to say he did what he could

He holds inside things
He should get out and let go
And talks too often
About his chosen broken road

In him, you will always find
A man trying to be just "a man"
A sound piece of mind
Reasons to stand

Your daddy, Son, is humbled
By a glance in your eyes
For God to choose him to raise you
He will always wonder why

Decisions are easily made
Remember this as you grow
It's how you choose to decide
In which your character will show

He prays to choose right
When it's you on the line
To keep you safe and teach you
To be strong, to be kind

A stronger will than he
A wiser soul indeed
If just one thing to pass on
The piece in you, The best in me.

—Johnny Joey Jones

Marines, I see as two breeds: Rottweilers or Dobermans. Because Marines come in two varieties: big and mean or skinny and mean. They're aggressive on the attack and tenacious on defense. They've got really short hair and they always go for the throat.

—RAdm. "Jay" R. Stark, USN; 10 November 1995

I have flown around the circumference of this world. I have fought two wars in some of the harshest environments imaginable. I have lived in other countries and taken great care to see their virtues. I can say with distinct certainty that America is the greatest country in the world. Not because we have the greatest military, or the largest wealth or even the freest form of government. No, those things are only effects of a greater cause. What makes this country so unique and so amazing is that we love one another, we help one another. We bind together not because of a similar ethnic origin or religious affiliation, but simply because through the shared sacrifice of our diverse forefathers, we are all Americans!

Staff Sergeant (Ret.)
Joey Jones, USMC EOD

Combat-wounded Staff Sergeant (Ret.) Johnny "Joey" Jones turned a traumatic, life-changing disability into a personal mission to improve the lives of all veterans. Known to his friends as "Triple J," Jones was raised in Dalton, GA and enlisted in the Marine Corps after high school. During his eight years of service, he worked as an Explosive Ordnance Disposal (bomb) Technician, deploying to both Iraq and Afghanistan on separate tours. During his last deployment to Afghanistan, Jones was responsible for disarming and destroying 80+ improvised explosive devices (IEDs) and thousands of pounds of other unknown bulk explosives. During that tour on August 6, 2010, he stepped on and initiated an IED, resulting in the loss of both of his legs above the knee and severe damage to his right forearm and both wrists. He recovered at Walter Reed National Military Medical Center in Washington D.C. Focusing on overcoming adversity, finding a positive perspective in dire situations, leaning on those around you, and finding strength in yourself and your community, Joey now serves at the Chief Spokesperson for Zac Brown's Southern Ground and Military director and spokesperson for Camp Southern Ground. Joey regularly appears as an outspoken, yet insightful military analyst for Fox News.

www.johnnyjoeyjones.com
www.facebook.com/JohnnyJoeyJones
www.instagram.com/johnny_joey

Test Page:

Made in the USA
San Bernardino, CA
24 May 2020

72287497R00033